I0417573

Saba's Unique Cloud Forest

and how it evolved following a series of major hurricanes

By

Tom van't Hof

Published by the author 2010

Copyright 2010 by Tom van't Hof

Introduction

When I first visited the cloud forest on top of Mt. Scenery back in the early eighties I don't think I had a clear sense of what I was looking at, but I did realize it was special. Of course, I tried to capture the magical atmosphere in photographs, but the forest was so dense that it seemed all but impossible. It wasn't until after hurricane Hugo in 1989 when the forest had become more open due to the storm's impact that I was able to penetrate deeper and photograph the majestic Mountain Mahogany trees with their long sprawling branches and luxuriant epiphytic[1] cover.

In December of 1989 Dr. Richard A. Howard, author of the Flora of the Lesser Antilles, emeritus professor at Harvard University and director of the Arnold Arboretum, visited Saba at the invitation of the Saba Conservation Foundation. It was Howard who made me aware how fragile, important and special the cloud forest on Mt. Scenery was. Howard passed away in 2003, but I am forever grateful for sharing his knowledge with me.

Over the years I have climbed up to the cloud forest numerous times (I have been a permanent resident in Saba since 1986) and camped there with my wife Heleen Cornet (an artist who draws inspiration for her paintings from the cloud forest). The more I explored, the more intrigued and passionate I became about the cloud forest. Between 1989 and 1999 Saba experienced the fury of four major hurricanes, an exceptional frequency and intensity. Following each hurricane I went up to see how the forest had fared. It made me aware of nature's resilience, because, apart from breakage of branches, defoliation and occasional uprooting of a large tree, the cloud forest recovered quickly and the large trees would be as lofty as ever within a month or two. Except in 1998.

[1]Epiphyte, from the Greek *epi*=on and *phyton*=plant: a plant that grows on another plant or tree.

While hurricane Georges in 1998 caused complete defoliation of the Mountain Mahogany and other trees, new leaves started sprouting quickly after the storm. However, a few months after the hurricane a relapse occurred. The Mountain Mahoganies began loosing their new leaves and eventually only a few survived. This was most baffling and I tried to entice specialists to come to Saba and help answering the question of what had happened. It seemed a unique opportunity for scientific research and monitoring. Unfortunately, to no avail. So I continued my own quasi-scientific monitoring and photographic documentation.

Since my observations of the cloud forest represent about the only knowledge available of the history of the cloud forest during a period of intense hurricanes, I decided that I should put my knowledge in writing before it gets lost. The result of that decision lies here before you.

What is a Cloud Forest?

While the official name for what I refer to as cloud forest in this booklet is "tropical montane cloud forest", you will find several other terms in the literature such as "misty forest", "mossy forest", and – because of the eerie impression of the tangled and dwarfed trees - "elfin forest", "elfin woodland", or "fairy forest".

Cloud forests are found at a range of elevations. They typically occur between 1,500 and 3,000 m above sea level, but may occur as low as 500 m on steep small island mountains. They are frequently covered in clouds or mist and are characterized by high humidity and rainfall. Considerable amounts of moisture are added by interception of water from the clouds on the vegetation (this is known as horizontal precipitation or cloud stripping). Temperature is reduced and the soils are waterlogged. Short, gnarled, twisted or stunted trees are typical for this forest type. Trees are covered with epiphytes, including mosses, liverworts, ferns, bromeliads, orchids, and other flowering plants. They are characterized by relatively high biodiversity and high endemism[2].

To summarize in popular terms: it's wet, muddy and misty most of the time. It can also be pretty cold and windy in cloud forests at higher elevations. While all of this doesn't sound very appealing, you still want to go there, because it's rich and very different from any other forest type you know.

The Setting

The island of Saba is located at 17°37' 30" North and 63°14' 30" West, or about 50 km South of St. Maarten in the Northeastern Caribbean. Saba is the northernmost island of the volcanic inner arc of the Lesser Antilles. It has a surface area of 12.5 sq. km and the highest point on Mt. Scenery is 872 m above sea level. The current population (2010) is nearing 2,000 inhabitants.

The island is essentially a dormant stratovolcano that was formed about 500,000 years ago. The volcano has a horseshoe-shaped structure that opens up to the Southwest, or roughly the area of The Bottom up to Troy Hill. This structure is due to a sector collapse that took place some 100,000 years ago. The summit of Mt. Scenery is a lava dome, which partially overlies the

[2]An endemic species is one that is native to a particular region and not found elsewhere.

sector collapse and is surrounded by numerous flank domes (such as Old Booby Hill, Maskehorne Hill, Great Hill, Paris Hill, etc.). The original crater has been filled in by pyroclastic (block and ash) deposits.

The most recent eruption has been dated to the year 1640, just prior to the first European settlement (Roobol and Smith, 2004). Roobol and Smith speculate that the first European settlers were attracted by grassy meadows in the area of The Bottom, which replaced mature forest that had been destroyed by the recent volcanic eruption. Current volcanic activity is exemplified by hot springs near Ladder Bay in the Southwest (temperature about 55° C) and near Green Island in the Northeast (temperature about 75° C) and by occasional tremors.

The climate is tropical and ranges from a savannah to monsoon climate. Humidity and rainfall increase considerably with elevation, while temperature drops. The average annual rainfall is about 1,100 mm and roughly one-third of this falls in the months of September through November. February, March and April are the driest months of the year. However, rainfall is erratic and there are considerable deviations from long-term averages in both annual and monthly rainfall. No data are available for the higher elevations, but it is quite possible that annual rainfall on the top of Mt. Scenery is around 2,000 mm. Since the summit of Mt. Scenery is enveloped in clouds most of the time, interception of cloud moisture by the foliage forms an important contribution to total rainfall.

Trunks and branches of the Mountain Mahogany trees are loaded with epiphytes

The Cloud Forest before 1998

The top of Mt. Scenery can best be portrayed as a series of valleys surrounded by steep ridges. In the center is a large valley[3], quite flat, with smaller valleys in the western area (to the left of the main trail as it enters the cloud forest) and towards the east (the area below the antenna tower). A third large elongated valley, running in an east-west direction is located on the northern side of the top. Most of the Mountain Mahogany trees are found on the ridges surrounding these valleys, in other words on the more exposed areas of the top. When the antenna tower was built a good-sized chunk of the cloud forest was cleared. According to those who worked there some old and large Mountain Mahogany trees were felled at the time and this area is still quite open and dry today.

Historical information about the cloud forest in Saba is scant. Dutch botanist A.L. Stoffers conducted a botanical investigation of the Netherlands Antilles in 1952 and 1953, the results of which were published as "The Vegetation of the Netherlands Antilles" (Stoffers, 1956). Stoffers described the cloud forest to be dominated by two species of trees, the Mountain Mahogany and Leathery Colicwood and characterized by low and gnarled trees, often forming an impenetrable growth up to 6 m high. Stoffers found the branches of the trees "laden with mosses and epiphytes, mainly ferns, but orchids are also present".

I once went to the top in the nineties accompanied by a forestry expert and, using a quick-and-dirty forestry technique, we established the tallest Mountain Mahogany trees to be 15 m high. This means that either those 6 m tall trees grew an additional 9 m in 40 years, or that Stoffers did not see the same things we saw. The former seems very unlikely[4]. The publication doesn't state exactly how much time Stoffers spent on Saba, but from the dates of his photographs we may conclude that he visited Saba and St. Eustatius during the period April to August 1953. That is not a lot of time for detailed descriptions of all the different types of vegetation occurring on the two islands. Somewhat surprisingly, Stoffers makes no mention of cultivated areas in the

Leaves of Mountain Mahogany (l) and Leathery Colicwood (r)

[3]Contrary to popular belief this not the crater, as the original crater has been filled in.
[4]The tallest Mountain Mahogany adjacent to the clearing that was made for the construction of the antenna tower can be a maximum of 40 years old and was only 6 m high in 2009.

central valley. Since Stoffers furthermore remarked that the vegetation of the cloud forest "…formed an often impenetrable growth….." it is likely that he has not been able to explore the cloud forest extensively.

Subsequent scientists who studied vegetation on Saba have mostly followed Stoffers' description (e.g. Augustinus, Mees and Prins, 1985; Rojer, 1997). It is not until 2006 that a comprehensive survey of the biodiversity of the island was initiated by Conservation International, with botanical collecting undertaken by the scientists of the New York Botanical Garden (Mori et al., 2007 onward). This study, which focused on inventory and did not describe vegetation types, was unfortunately discontinued due to lack of funding.

As mentioned earlier, Dr. Richard A. Howard visited Saba in 1989 and I had the privilege to explore the cloud forest with him. Howard called the Mountain Mahogany the "feature tree" of Saba's cloud forest. He emphasized that the name is rather unfortunate, as it suggests a relationship to the West Indian Mahogany and a similar use of its wood. The Mountain Mahogany belongs in the tea family and is more closely related to the camellias, while its wood is not useful. The Mountain Mahogany is endemic to the Lesser Antilles and Saba is the northernmost point of its distribution.

As companion plants Howard mentions the Trumpetwood tree and the Leathery Colicwood. He also says that the Saba cloud forest is not "elfin" (the trees are not really dwarfed) nor a proper "mossy forest" because the epiphytic layer is dominated by leafy liverworts, filmy ferns and many other ferns. Howard mentions two unusual flowering epiphytes, Guadalupe Wild Coffee and a Bladderwort species, a carnivorous plant that traps insects. The plant has an orchid-like flower and should be protected.

Most importantly, Howard recognized the unique character and the hydrological importance of the Saba cloud forest. To quote: "The elfin forest on Saba is unlike that on any other island in the Caribbean and deserves special recognition and protection" (Howard, 1990). And another quote: "The epiphytic vegetation on tree branches and on the forest floor is essentially a sponge which is the water reservoir for all forests and cultivated plants below it in elevation. Remove the sponge reservoir and the terraced gardens that depend on it cannot survive" (Howard, 1990).

In 2003 I presented a poster on the Saba cloud forest and the hurricane impact at a forestry conference in Puerto Rico. Two cloud forest experts assured me that they had never seen anything like it, with the possible exception of one of the cloud forests in Central America (but without the Mountain Mahogany, of course).

Just to make sure there is no misunderstanding about why the cloud forest on Saba is different:
1.The Mountain Mahogany is the "signature tree" in Saba, while it is uncommon or absent in other cloud forests.
2.Trees are much taller in Saba compared to other cloud forests (up to 15 m in Saba as opposed to 4-6 m in other Caribbean cloud forests).

Flower of epiphytic Bladderwort species (endemic to the Caribbean). This carnivorous plant has tubers and roots with insect traps

The reason for these differences remains the object of speculation. I think it may well have to do with differences in elevation and climatic conditions. Saba's cloud forest is located at an elevation of 825-870 m, while the other Caribbean cloud forest are typically at much higher elevations where climatic conditions are much more extreme. Higher wind speeds in particular may be responsible for dwarfed tree growth in other cloud forests.

It's time now to sum up the botanical information on the cloud forest prior to 1998 available in the literature, supplemented with my own observations.
•Mountain Mahogany is the "signature tree", growing primarily on the exposed ridges.
•Companion trees include Leathery Colicwood and Trumpetwood.
•Also common are the West Indian Treefern, Muricate Treefern and one species of palm tree, the Mountain Cabbage.
•In the shrub layer we find Mountain Fuchsia, White Bell, Lobsterclaw, and Giant Elephant Ear.
•In the ground layer are many species of ferns, a Begonia (Mountain Manna), Besleria lutea (no common name known), an Anthurium (Organ Mountain Laceleaf), Bromeliads, and several species of ground orchids, including the Hairy Shadow Witch, Caribbean False Helmet Orchid, and Bog Orchid. One tiny parasitic[5] plant with small yellow flowers, the Leafless Ghostplant, is found on decaying wood.

[5] The relationship is called myco-heterotrophy, whereby the plant gets all or part of its food from fungi rather than through photosynthesis.

•Climbers and epiphytes are abundant. Many epiphytes are also growing terrestrially. Two flowering epiphytes endemic to the Caribbean are found, Guadalupe Wild Coffee and a carnivorous Bladderwort species. The epiphytic Flame Orchid is present, but not common.
•Mosses and liverworts are a very important element of the flora.
The valleys contain many of the same elements, but differ in the sense that they lack the Mountain Mahogany, have few Leathey colicwood trees, and comparatively more Trumpetwood and Mountain Fuchsia. Here we also find Pepper species[6].

Clockwise from top left: Mountain Fuchsia, Guadalupe Wild Coffee (endemic to the Caribbean), epiphytic Flame Orchid, and flowering Bromeliad

[6] Species in the Piper family, not to be confused with the edible peppers of the Potato family.

Clockwise from top left: Mountain Manna, *Besleria lutea*, Caribbean false helmetorchid, and Trumpetwood tree

Mountain cabbage (l) with sheathed flower (r)
Bottom: rich epiphytic growth on Mt. Mahogany

Above: epiphytic mosses and ferns. Below: Epidendrum orchid (l) and Treeferns (r)

Lobsterclaw

Giant Eelephant ear and flower

Trees in the tropics don't show growth rings

Age and Development of the Cloud Forest

The cloud forest on Saba is considered a climax community. Imagine that a bare surface becomes available for colonization by plants, the vegetation will go through several stages (a process called succession), whereby more complex communities gradually replace earlier, simpler communities. Eventually a quasi-equilibrium, or climax, is reached, which represents the final collection of plant species that are best adapted to the climatic and soil conditions of the area. You could say that it is the "final expression" of that particular type of vegetation. A climax state could presumably remain forever, or until a major disturbance takes place.

In temperate zones trees show growth rings or annual rings, which represent a faster growth during the summer and a slowdown during the winter. Such rings can be used to determine the age of trees. In the absence of distinct summer and winter seasons in the tropics, trees in tropical climates do not develop these annual rings and determination of age is not possible. In other words, we don't have a clue as to how old the Mountain Mahogany trees could be. However, I'm willing to stick my neck out and say that the oldest trees were at least 300 to 400 years old. I'm tempted to put the age estimate even higher than that, but the last volcanic eruption was dated to the early 17th century. This eruption didn't necessarily take place at the top and could well have been local, somewhere below the top. But there is no way to establish this without extensive research.

My guess is based mostly on gut feeling, but to some extent also on more rational considerations. For example, some of the large trees had a 1 m diameter. Seedlings and saplings grow quickly in height in the first decades, but at some point growth in height will slow down considerably as more energy is applied to growth in girth and development of the sprawling branches. And finally, the wood is quite compact.

Past Natural and Human Impacts

We don't know much about past natural impacts, but we can be sure that past tropical storms and hurricanes have impacted to various degrees on the cloud forest. More recently, between 1989 and 1999 Saba has experienced five hurricanes (three category-3 or higher and one category-2; see box).

Year	Name	Category	Wind speed at minimum distance to Saba		
			Knots	Miles per hour	Km per hour
1989	Hugo	4	121	140	224
1995	Luis	4	125	145	232
1995	Marilyn[7]	2	82	95	152
1998	Georges	3	100	115	184
1999	Lenny	3-4	100-115	115-132	184-211

Following each of these hurricanes I have gone up the mountain to look at the damage inflicted. The impact of a major hurricane (category-3 and up) can best be described as follows:
•Complete or almost complete defoliation.
•Flattening of most of the undergrowth.
•Topping of treeferns and palm trees.
•Extensive breakage.
•Some uprooting of trees.
It was surprising to see that very few large Mountain Mahogany trees were uprooted as a result of these hurricanes. Some of the uprooted trees revealed that they had a shallow root system and that they had been growing on top of big boulders with their roots enclosing the boulder.

We know of some human activities that have impacted on the cloud forest:
•In the past people did farm on the top of the mountain, but this was probably done only in the flat valleys. You can still find huge banana trees and Tannia[8] plants in the central valley, and an occasional Tannia in the valley below the antenna tower.
•The Mt. Scenery step road, part of which runs through the cloud forest, was completed in 1964.
•A sizeable portion of the cloud forest was cleared for the construction of the transmitting tower which was completed around 1972.

[7] Although Marilyn was a lesser hurricane it hit only 10 days after Luis, hardly enough for any recovery of nature.
[8] Scientific name Xanthosama sagittifolium, also know as Yautia or Dasheen. The closely related Taro (Colocasia esculenta), also known as Eddoe or Dasheen is also found on Saba and both are cultivated for their starchy tuberous corms.

Hurricane damage: a tangled mass of broken branches

A sizeable portion of the cloud forest was
Cleared for the construction of the antenna
Tower in 1972

Tannia plant, testimony to past agriculture

Hurricane Georges: End of a Climax and a New Beginning

On September 21st 1998 hurricane Georges hit Saba with maximum sustained winds of 100 knots[9]. The highest wind speed during the passage of Georges in the Caribbean was actually from an unofficial report received from Saba. It was a gust of 153 knots at an elevation of about 210 m (Guiney, 1999a). Needless to say that there was extensive damage to property and to nature.

I went up to the top of Mt. Scenery within a week after the passing of Georges. My preliminary survey indicated that there was complete defoliation, nearly all of the undergrowth was flattened, extensive breakage of tree branches, and some uprooting of trees. Many of the large Mountain Mahogany trees had been stripped of their epiphytic growth, at least on the side of the trunk where they had been exposed to the wind. Even some bark stripping took place. The forest was more open than I had ever seen it before. Overall a sinister picture.

Abovet: skeletons of Mountain mahogany trees 3 years after hurricane Georges

Left: bark stripping

But, like after previous hurricanes, nature showed its usual resilience and recovery set in quickly. In the first months after the hurricane the Mountain Mahogany trees were sprouting new leaves and it seemed as if recovery was proceeding in the same way as I had seen after previous storms. Then something weird happened. Most of the old Mountain Mahogany trees started to shed their new leaves! I had no clue as to what was happening.

[9] 1 knot = 1.85 km/hr = 1.15 mile/hr

By the middle of 1999 an estimated 75 to 85% of the Mountain Mahogany trees were leafless and apparently dead, although I still found it hard to accept that they had really died. By mid-November 1999 hurricane Lenny, another category-4 storm weakening to category 3 as it passed Saba, approached the island from the West (an unusual phenomenon). It lingered very close to the island for two days. A gust of 145 knots was recorded in Saba before the anemometer blew away (Guiney, 1999b). Although some believe that Lenny dealt the final blow to the cloud forest, it is evident that the large-scale mortality among the Mountain Mahogany was actually the result of Georges. By mid-2000 I concluded that nearly 100% of the Mountain Mahogany trees were dead. I was able to find two surviving trees, that is, in the more easily accessible part of the cloud forest.

In April 2001 I did not find any seedlings of the Mountain Mahogany. My original fear that the openness of the cloud forest would cause the soils to dry out was unfounded. First of all, the stripped moss cover from the trees formed a protective layer on the ground and secondly, hurricanes Lenny and Jose[10] brought lots of rain. Although a new and dense shrub layer was forming rapidly, the forest seemed to be dominated by towering skeletons of the dead Mountain Mahogany. It was too depressing for me to go to the top for a while and I was also really busy with other work, traveling a lot of the time.

Above: sapling of Mountain Mahogany

Left: young Mountain Cabbage

[10] Hurricane Jose was a category-2 hurricane that passed north of Saba on October 21st 1999.

New growth of Trumpetwood tree (l) and West Indian Treefern (r)

But then in March 2003 I counted 18 young saplings of the Mountain Mahogany on a very superficial survey in the northwestern section of the cloud forest. The tallest of these were about 1.80 m high. Apparently the open character of the forest, combined with abundant rainfall in late 1999, had created favorable conditions for germination of Mountain Mahogany seeds that must have been plentiful in the soil. My depression began to wane and renewed interest was formed. I took up photographic monitoring again of recovery in a spot I had marked right after hurricane Georges and of some prominent skeletons and one of the surviving Mountain Mahogany trees. Eventually I identified about four old surviving Mountain Mahogany trees[11].

The recovery pattern not only showed a rapid re-growth of the shrub layer, also the tree layer gradually began to recover. Apart from the saplings of the Mountain Mahogany, other trees also re-appeared.

Rather than giving you a dull summation of species let me take you into the forest for a unique experience of both past and present.

We're going off the main trail as it enters the cloud forest, on the first side track to the left. Be prepared, it's going to be muddy and slippery, but worth every step of the way. On the ground we will see white orchids (they bloom around the months of January and February). To our left

[11] I can't be conclusive here because one is in an inaccessible area. Since it can only be seen from a distance it could be more than one tree.

we have the southwestern valley. All around us are Treeferns and Mountain Cabbage palms. Look for their long flower spikes with tiny white flowers. Along the track will be some Mountain Fuchsia shrubs with their bright red blossoms. Then we will see the saplings of the Leathery Colicwood trees and the Mountain Mahogany. You may not be able to distinguish them at first, but the Mountain Mahogany leaves are fringed, undulate, as the scientific name indicates. We see skeletons of old Mountain Mahogany trees, as a testimony of past grandeur. Then, as the track begins to turn to the left, look over to your right to see one of the remaining old Mountain Mahogany trees behind the shrubs in the foreground. There is one tree that has two species of epiphytic orchids, including the Flame orchid, but their exact location is better not disclosed, since orchids tend to disappear mysteriously, as more people know of their location. The track turns back to the right again, you have to bend down to cross a large tree, and you will see some large old Mountain Mahogany trees that, even though they are no longer alive, still have all their epiphytic growth fully intact. You have arrived in a magical world. Just stand there for a few minutes, look around you and let it all sink in. One of the trees has the Bladderwort species and the Guadalupe Wild Coffee among the epiphytes on its branches. Another 10 minutes and you will be at the Wells Bay top, but if it is totally clouded it's not worth the effort, because there will be no view from the top and you have already seen the very best.

One of the few surviving old Mountain Mahogany trees

Old Mountain Mahogany trees with their epiphytic growth still fully intact

As I mentioned before the Mountain Mahogany trees are found mostly on the exposed ridges rather than in the valleys. The valleys seemed to have fared much better. This is understandable as the wind is being pushed up along the ridges and wind speeds accelerate, whereas the valleys are more protected (insofar as one can speak of "protected" during a category-3 or 4 storm in such a small area). I did not pay the same amount of attention to the valleys as to the ridges after hurricane Georges, but I certainly have the impression that they survived much more intact. The central valley, of course, already contained introduced elements of flora because of past farming, but the valley below the tower certainly looked almost pristine.

The big question remaining is what happened and why? What caused the end of the climax and why did it happen in 1998? The short answer lies in last part of the definition of climax state: "A climax state could presumably remain forever, or until a major disturbance takes place". A category-3 or 4 hurricane certainly is a major disturbance. Yes, you will say, but it survived other major hurricanes before! Perhaps historical data can give us further clues as to whether a similar frequency of intense hurricanes has affected Saba in the past. We have not had good, reliable hurricane data for a very long time, as hurricane hunters have been flying into storms only since 1944 and the first weather satellite came into orbit in 1960. However, through re-analysis of past data, experts have constructed tropical storm and

Magical mossy forest in the valley below the antenna tower

hurricane tracks from 1851 onwards (UNISYS, 2009)[12]. I looked for clusters of 3 or more major storms (category-3 and higher) that came to within roughly 100 km[13] of Saba during a 10-year time span and only found one cluster between 1922 to 1932 that fitted those criteria.

In other words, if the frequency and intensity of hurricanes is the main factor controlling the life of the climax state, we have only seen one major disturbance since 1851 similar to that of 1989-1998. Although there will never be conclusive evidence, I do believe that the age of the Mountain Mahogany trees, combined with the frequency and intensity of the hurricanes during the period 1989-1998 provides the best answer to the question why the current climax ended in 1998. I have often used the parallel with a town where a comparatively large number of elderly people live. Imagine two really bad winters in a row and then also a flu epidemic during the second winter. What happens? Many of these older folks don't make it through the second winter. The Saba cloud forest was in a climax state and most of its Mountain Mahogany trees were pretty old. It experienced three major and one category-2 hurricane in 10 years time. That was just one too many. Instead of thinking of a climax state as a stable state, or "one that could presumably remain forever" as the definition states, we might want to think in terms of cycles of development in the case of a cloud forest like Saba where major disturbances are not infrequent. But if these cycles can be hundreds of years long, as I suggested earlier, then you may really consider it a "historic moment" if you happen to be there when the end of a cycle occurs and a new beginning takes place.

It still remains puzzling why initial recovery of the Mountain Mahogany trees took place after hurricane Georges. The question will probably never be answered satisfactorily, but since I noticed the shallow rooting of many trees, I speculated that the fury of the storms caused substantive root damage (those trees will have been shaken severely by the wind), which eventually prevented the trees from taking up enough water and nutrients from the soil. They tried with some degree of success, but it wasn't enough and eventually they gave up. Some people suggested that the stripping of the epiphytic cover played a role in the mortality, but I have not been able to find any evidence in the literature for direct uptake of water and nutrients from epiphytes. And not all trees that died were stripped of their epiphytic layer.

Land Tenure and Conservation Status

Land tenure is not a simple matter on Saba. Most of the land is privately owned and only a portion has been surveyed and registered. The top of Mt. Scenery is presumably Government land, because Cable and Wireless leased the section where the transmitting tower was built from Government and because the people who used to farm there paid rent to Government.

[12] While earlier hurricane data is available (Meteorological Service Netherlands Antilles and Aruba, 2009), it is difficult to analyze as no wind speeds are available for storms prior to 1851.
[13] The 100 km distance is somewhat arbitrary. The idea is to use the distance to which hurricane force winds extend from the center of the storm, but this may vary considerably and depends on the size of the hurricane. The hurricanes of 1989-1999 all came to within a distance of 100 km.

Following Howard's visit to Saba, the Saba Conservation Foundation advocated the establishment of a forest reserve that would afford full protection to the cloud forest on the top of the Mountain. The Cadastral Office prepared a certificate for the land above 820 m and the Government was asked to claim this land through a so-called prescriptive rights procedure. This has never been implemented and to this date the cloud forest does not have any protected status. Considering the biological and hydrological importance of the cloud forest, I hope that the Government will take up the original proposal by the Saba Conservation Foundation so that this unique resource will be safeguarded for future generations.

Literature Cited

Augustinus, P.G.E.F, R.P.R Mees and M. Prins (Eds.). 1985. Biotic and Abiotic Components of the Landscapes of Saba (Netherlands Antilles). Report of an integrated Research into the Botany and Physical Geography. Uitgaven Natuurwetenschappelijke Studiekring voor Suriname en de Nederlandse Antillen, no 115.

Guiney, John L. 1999a. Preliminary Report Hurricane Georges, 15 September to 01 October 1998. National Hurricane Center. http://www.nhc.noaa.gov/1998georges.html

Guiney, John L. 1999b. Preliminary Report Hurricane Lenny, 12 – 23 November 1999. National Hurricane Center. http://www.nhc.noaa.gov/1999lenny.html

Howard, R.A. 1990. Saba, the Unspoiled Queen. Wildflower 6(4):34-49.

Meteorological Service Netherlands Antilles and Aruba. 2009. http://www.weather.an/reports/documents/HurricanesandTropicalStorms.pdf

Mori, S. A., W. R. Buck, C. A. Gracie & M. Tulig. 2007 onward. Plants and Lichens of Saba (http://sweetgum.nybg.org/saba/). Virtual Herbarium of The New York Botanical Garden.

Rojer, A. 1997. Biologische Inventarisatie van Saba. KNAP project 96-10. Stichting Carmabi, Curacao.

Roobol, J. and A.L. Smith. 2004. Volcanology of Saba and St. Eustatius. Koninklijke Nerderlands Akademie van Wetenschappen.

Stoffers, A.L. 1956. Sudies on the Flora and Fauna of Curacao and Other Caribbean Islands. Volume I. The Vegetation of the Netherlands Antilles. Uitgaven Natuurwetenschappelijke Studiekring voor Suriname en de Nederlandse Antillen. No. 15.

UNISYS. 2009. http://weather.unisys.com/hurricane/atlantic/index.html

List of common and scientific names

Common Name	Scientific name
Bladderwort species	*Utricularia alpina*
Bog Orchid	*Habenaria sp.*
Caribbean False Helmet Orchid	*Erythrodes plantaginea*
Flame Orchid	*Maxillaria coccinea*
Giant Bell	*Hillia parasitica*
Giant Elephant Ear	*Philodendron giganteum*
Guadalupe Wild Coffee	*Psychotria guadalupensis*
Hairy Shadow Witch	*Ponthieva racemosa*
Leafless Ghostplant	*Voyria aphylla*
Leathery Colicwood	*Myrsine coriacea*
Lobtserclaw	*Heliconia caribaea*
Mountain Cabbage	*Prestoea acuminata var. montana*
Mountain Fuchsia	*Charianthus crinitus*
Mountain Mahogany	*Freziera undulata*
Mountain Manna	*Begonia obliqua*
Muricate Treefern	*Cyathea muricata*
Organ Mountain Laceleaf	*Anthurium cordatum*
Pepper	*Piper spp.*
Trumpetwood	*Cecropia schreberiana*
West Indian Mahogany	*Swietenia mahogani*
West Indian Treefern	*Cyathea arborea*

Acknowledgment

I am very grateful to Paul Illsley (Centre of Geographic Sciences, Nova Scotia, Canada) for producing a detailed map of the top of Mt. Scenery for this booklet. Paul has conducted extensive GPS surveys of the island to map the exact location of trails. Thanks are also due to Janine LeSueur and Rik Lina for sharing some of their photographs with me. Kathy Freeland gave her blessing to the manuscript. And finally, my wife, Heleen Cornet, critically read the manuscript and gave her usual invaluable artistic input in the design and layout of this booklet.

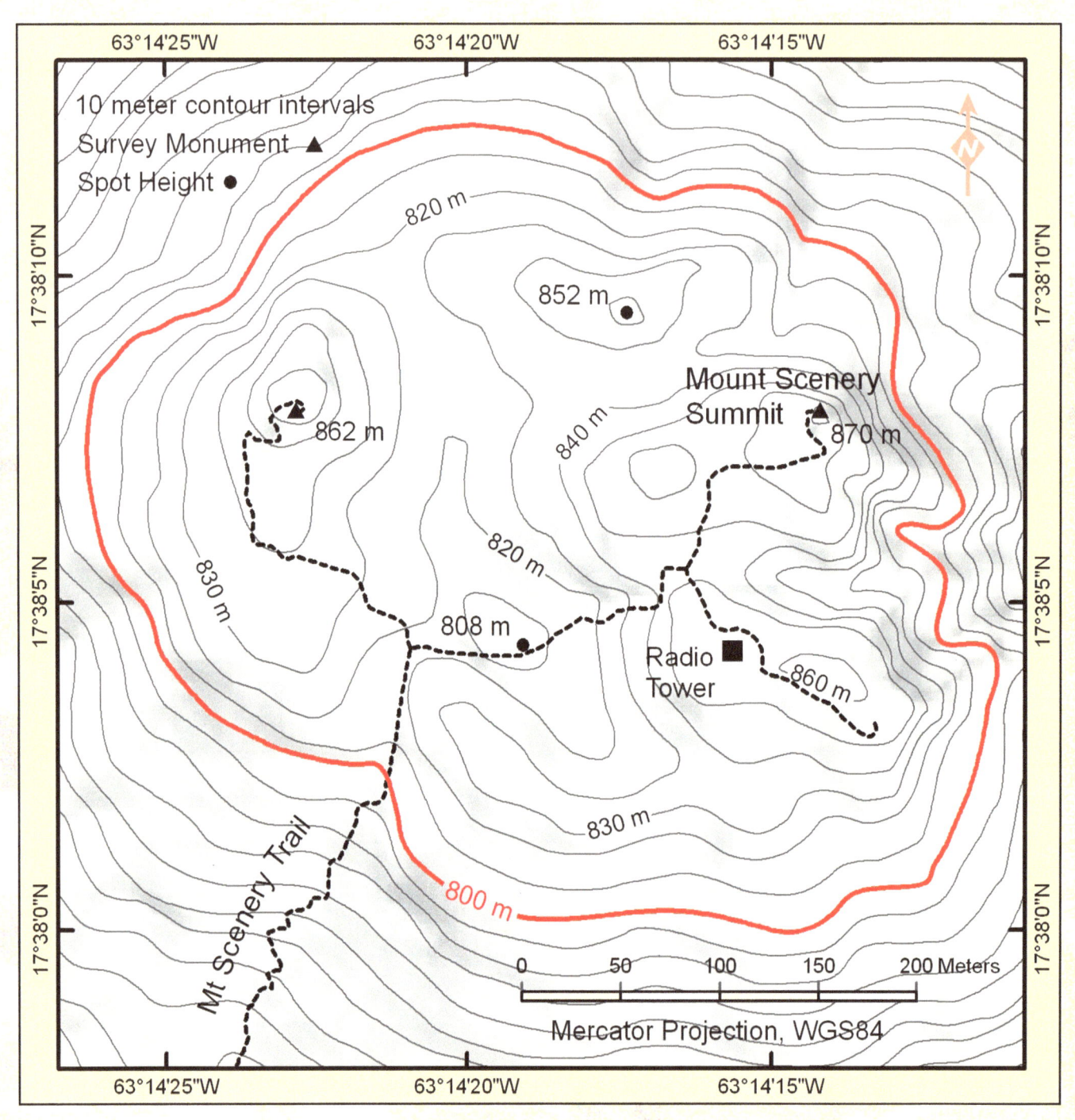

The Magical Mossy Rainforest
Watercolor on canvas 3 x 4 ft
Heleen Cornet

www.ingramcontent.com/pod-product-compliance
Lightning Source LLC
Chambersburg PA
CBHW040309010626
45792CB00025B/1719